HE COMES FIRST:

How to make your man feel loved

Melissa A. Beaver

Table Of Contents

Introduction

In reality, love is getting to know someone's face, observing how their eyes light up when they're happy, figuring out how they want to be touched whether they're happy, upset or turned on, and figuring out how to handle disagreements together.

James M. Sama compiled a humorous list of tips for men on how to please women and what simple things they like. The same, in my opinion, applies to men. And whether you're married or just started seeing someone, if you have a nice man to love, he deserves to feel the same way about you.

1. Give him praise.

Where did we obtain the idea that only women enjoy hearing compliments on their appearance, scent, level of intelligence, or sexiness?

I've always believed that men are more assured of their physical attractiveness and sex appeal than women are. Guys are supposed to be unconcerned with things like their appearance or if their new haircut looks good.

What BS that is! I've never encountered a man who didn't give a damn about how gorgeous he believed he was to the woman he loved. Tell him when you see him, and just feel the sensation of "Oh my gosh, you are so sexy."

It's simple: whenever it occurs to you, tell him the nice stuff. Tell him that despite his worn-out, worn-in tee shirt, he still looks gorgeous. Tell him how much you enjoy hugging him and sniffing his neck.

2. Express your gratitude to him for all that he does for you and the family.

If your partner has a job outside the home, express your gratitude to him. Even if he adores his job, I can almost promise that he has days when he considers quitting, screaming at his boss, or just spending the entire day in his office. He doesn't, though. You and your family might be a contributing factor.

Anyone who earns a living has a tremendous responsibility, but society stresses this for males more than women. Sadly, their ability to earn is frequently correlated with how important they are to our culture. As bad as it may be, it only gets worse when we fail to acknowledge the strain and effort guys are putting themselves through.

Your partner is making sacrifices for your family if he is working from home when the kids are present. Even though he presumably enjoys being the stay-at-home parent tremendously, all parents experience moments when they want to give up (or change a diaper), scream at the boss (the baby?), or hide in a dark place. However, they don't! They spend the entire day looking after the kids at such a place, elbow-deep in something disgusting.

It's simple: Just let him know that you are aware of how challenging his work might be. Inform him that you value it and that you recognize his dedication. It doesn't matter if it's your money or his; what matters is that you acknowledge something that most people take for granted.

3. Give the bedroom some time to heat up.

No, he's probably not a sex god, but keep your sex intense and sacred for both of you since the finest sex feels transcendent, reciprocal, connected, steamy, and dreamy. It will probably make both of your lives happier if you make him feel like your own personal sex deity and he does the same for you.

Nobody ever owes their spouse sex, but in a healthy relationship, fostering desire is a good thing. Try spending the night in a hotel room if you find it difficult to enter the sex-god or goddess mood at home. If that is out of your price range, camping in the woods may also be a lot of fun. If it suits you, you can discuss dreams or share erotic images like the varied collection in Dr. Timaree's NSFW library even at home.

You could also photograph yourself in a boudoir. Not feeling like getting too risqué or displaying your entire body? Try getting close-up shots of a sexually appealing but less visible body feature. The top of your underwear is showing through the hip pocket of your jeans and your bra strap is on your shoulder. There are many inspiring ideas available.

Nurturing your desire for him is an easy solution. You can decide to daydream about him, about a time you spent together, or about your favorite area of his body. When you next have a chance to be alone with him, shower him with all your passion.

4. Encourage him to spend time by himself.

Sincerity dictates that this was the hardest for me. I'm not sure why, but when Ivan and I first started dating, I disliked how much time he spent mountain biking or surfing.

We didn't see each other very much because we were both working, and I felt ignored.

That was unfair to place so much strain on my husband. We gradually figured out how to organize our alone time, and I took advantage of his encouragement of my desire for alone time to exercise, write, or simply read a book in bed.

Your separation is a good thing unless he is so engrossed in his alone time that you fall off his list of priorities. If you're concerned about how long he'll be gone, simply schedule his return and make plans for later with him at that time. When he uses his alone time for exercise or meditation, he'll likely be happier and healthier for having done it, and being apart can give you more to talk about.

It's simple: When he claims he's going off to do the things that bring him happiness alone, smile. He deserves a kiss. He'll feel supported, heard, and seen.

Part 1:

Non Sextual Ways To Make Your Man Feel Loved

Chapter 1

Know His Love Language

We make use of various words of affirmation, quality time, gifts, acts of service, and physical touch as our love languages to express and receive love. To be in a loving relationship with your partner, you don't have to speak the same love language to him, but you both need to understand what makes him feel appreciated.

To respond to your man's emotional requirements, you must be aware of his love language.

Is it even more important to have a mutual love language if you desire to rekindle a relationship with an ex? If yes, how can you develop this love language to strengthen your relationship?

Let's first examine the theory of love languages, which was created by American novelist Gary Chapman, before answering that query. In essence, according to Chapman, there are five distinct ways to give and receive love:

Words of affirmation,
Quality time,
Gifts,
Acts of service and ,
Physical touch.

It is crucial to talk about how you both express and receive love because it is likely that you and your man do not share the same love language.

Everybody expresses love uniquely, and we all have preferences for how we want to be loved. By understanding your man's love language, you can fully understand his emotional requirements and vice versa.

In the early stages of a relationship, we are excellent at expressing our gratitude to our partners. But over time, we cease expressing our affection because we start to take it for granted. The truth is that we require constant validation and appreciation from our spouses.

Although it's a common misconception, men don't always treat women the same way they do. While the ways we wish to receive love are more influenced by how we feel about ourselves, our ways of offering love may be taught behaviors. However, our partners may not always be aware of the latter.

Can a relationship between two people who have different love languages succeed?

Yes, two people who speak different love languages can communicate extremely effectively, just like two people who speak Chinese and English can. All we need to communicate is awareness and a desire to do so.

For instance, if one spouse values 'acts of service,' then doing things like grocery shopping to give them more time to do other things will be appreciated. However, if the other person perceives them as being routine activities that should be carried out in a partnership, the recipient will not feel appreciated.

A person who expresses love by physical touch is therefore open to public demonstrations of affection, even in front of huge crowds. In a more sensual sense, it implies they enjoy massages, snuggling, kissing, and other forms of physical contact. It also means they will become concerned if there is a lack of physical touch.

However, "words of affirmation" are a well-known love language, so give your lover extra compliments if you are not a sentimental person. The use of "words of affirmation" might also take the form of encouragement, love letters, or a specially curated music mix.

You can also use your voice in bed to communicate pleasure and let your lover know how fantastic they make you feel during private moments.

There's a significant probability your partner's love language is giving gifts if they enjoy purchasing stuff for other people.

It is an opportunity to resume the relationship with a completely fresh strategy when couples reunite after a protracted separation. By establishing clear standards and demands and articulating what each partner requires to feel loved, they can lay a new foundation. Couples can make extremely specific requests of their partner when they have a firm awareness of their partner's primary and secondary love languages, especially if they have examples of times when they may not have been particularly valued in the past.

As cliche as it may sound, learning to communicate openly is essential to a strong, healthy, and loving relationship because we all have different life experiences and, consequently, expectations.

Simple ways to show love to your man

- Hold his hands as often as possible

- Give him hugs before leaving and when returning home

- If he is sad, hold him closely to increase their oxytocin level

- Offer massages on a regular basis

- Play with his body

- Cuddle in bed before falling asleep

- Touch him on the arm or hold his hand while he is talking

- Dance together

Chapter 2

How To Make Your Man Feel Special With Texts And Words

Making someone you love smile is the best feeling in the world. It might brighten your day to know that your comments gave them a moment of joy.

You might want to learn how to make him feel special over text and with what you say to him, whether you're married or just starting to date.

He might smile at the charming things in your message, or he might swoon at the romantic poetry you included.

Here are some phrases you might use to express your affection for him:

Sending him a text message of love

It's never easy to be separated from a partner, but texts can keep your boyfriend close and connected. Even the worst day can be improved by receiving a love note.

<u>Here are a few messages that will make him smile:</u>

Hey sweetheart, I already miss you. I'm looking forward to seeing you when you return home after a successful day at work.

I adore you thousand times over. When I think about you, my heart is racing out of my chest. Go get 'em, my dashing man, today! I'm so proud of what you're accomplishing. I adore you a lot!

My favorite person is you. You have my undying love. I hope your day at work today is going great. You have my undying love.

You're kind, astute, and humorous. I hope you understand how proud I am of you; you have what it takes to realize all of your wildest aspirations.

I can't stop fluttering in my chest as I wait for you to finish work.

They get to keep you from 9 to 5, but I get to keep you forever.

I'm also busy today. Currently, I'm praising all of my lucky stars for bringing you into my life. Baby, I love you.

Even before you left this morning, I already started missing you.

I need a kiss right now. soon return home.

The ideal husband or boyfriend that a lady might have is you.

Did you know that every time your name appears on the screen of my phone, I still get excited? I hope it's you when I hear it buzz every time.

Everything you put your mind to, you succeed magnificently.

You laughing is one of my favorite sounds. Your arms encircling me is my favorite sensation.

I have so many favorite things about you that I could write a book about.

WORDS to calm your boyfriend down after a stressful day:

After a long day, there are various methods to cheer up a man. One of the options you have at your disposal to help him feel relieved after a difficult day is to express your love, support, and appreciation with some romantic notes.

When it comes to emotional feelings, men tend to present themselves as hardcore. This should not, however, prevent you, a lady, from sending him texts of gratitude and calming him.

Having a companion by your side during this time will lessen the impact of the pressure.

See some wonderful consoling phrases you can use to communicate with your loved ones.

No matter what, I'm available to you day or night! I wish to assist. Tell me what you require. Everyone would do it if it were simple. But you are not just any person, and this is not simple! I am aware of your busy schedule. Considering you

Remember that taking a break is acceptable.
I care about being here. I wish I could assist you in lifting the weight. Whatever happens, I will always be proud of you because I am so happy for you.

You are extremely adored and valued. There is a huge crowd supporting you.

I appreciate you entrusting me with your emotions. Do you have any further information to share? I'm rooting for you because I adore you. I'm confident you can overcome this.

It's not just you. I have your back. I adore you for a variety of reasons. That won't alter regardless of how this issue turns out. For you, this is nothing new. You can do this. Your current emotions are very understandable. I'm paying attention and I care.

Please take a moment to think about your past successes.

Writing or using kind words is crucial for establishing a strong connection and providing him the best chance to realize how much you value him. Always write in a way that speaks to the reader's heart, and your words should be sincere.

You should always send him heartfelt messages of love, in both joyful and sad times. Every time you express your love to him through heartfelt messages, a new desire is sparked within him, making him want to appreciate you even more. Furthermore, your union will be strong and long-lasting.

Part 2:

Sexual Ways To Make Your Man Feel Loved

Chapter 3

Spicy Sex Moves Men Crave In Bedroom

It's acceptable for you to occasionally take actions that will make your man happy. Most men don't actually need to ask for anything because they are usually very predictable in bed. However, if you're curious about what a man really needs and wants in bed, this is the place to find out.

Here are some bedtime essentials for men that will make them feel attracted to you.

1. He wants you to demonstrate your enjoyment for him.

Men learn very largely through visual means. Show him how you feel about it by showing him with your hands. According to

Vanessa Geffrard, spokesman for Lovers adult health brand and retailer, "don't be scared to move his hands, position your body, and use verbal and nonverbal communication to create a nice time for you both." Laying on the bed and touching yourself while telling him to gaze but not touch is a sexy role-playing technique. a fun, sexy method of telling and showing).

2. He desires to remove it from the bedroom.

Men enjoy diversity. Jacqueline Misla, sex expert and COO of Curious Fox, a community for the polyamory-curious, advises keeping things interesting by discovering new areas to play, such as the kitchen table, laundry room, and in the car, or even outside. "Having sex in unfamiliar places can also result in more enjoyable and imaginative roleplaying opportunities."

3. Sometimes, men want you to take the lead.

Although most men are happy to take the initiative, there are instances when they truly like to see you do so. This is so because men adore seeing their female partners excited for sex. They feel more confident as a result of this. Men who praise your initiative also signify that they would adore it if you were the one to suggest novel sex positions to attempt. Try new positions with your man right away because you now know he enjoys them. Whether the experiment is a success or a failure, your boyfriend will be pleased and grateful that you took the initiative.

4. They enjoy it when you use foul language

Now, some women take this literally and rant endlessly about the most trivial aspects of sex. Men do not prefer that. Men enjoy it when you interject a few naughty and sexy words during sex. You'll be astonished by how easily your man gets sexy. Even only the phrase "harder" is sufficient. It will perform miracles. Just be careful not to go all technical on him when you talk nasty. I am so wet, Baby, keep going, and It feels so fantastic are some phrases that will work wonders.

5. When women take charge in bed, they love it.

Yes, men do enjoy being in charge in bed, but have you ever wondered what may happen if you take the lead? Whatever transpires, he'll be much happier and more excited as a result. Nothing is more seductive than a woman who commands the bed and initiates all sex gestures. It doesn't imply that you beat him up with whips and belts made of leather. All you have to do is forcefully throw him into the bed while you are on top and pin his arms. This is enough to make a man lose his composure. Just having some naughty conversations can make this more sultry.

Additionally, when you surprise them in bed, they completely lose it.

When it comes to sex, try not to be too predictable. In terms of sex, men enjoy surprise just as much as you do. Like pinning him to the love unexpectedly and starting to make out, or surprising him with an early morning blow job. These are the types of surprises we're referring to. Additionally, you can engage in new sex positions and perform actions he believed you to detest. You might also take things a step further and treat him to a surprise erotic dance while wearing some truly seductive underwear. Surprise him frequently and see how his desire for you increases.

6. Be prepared to comply with any requests he makes.

Men truly desire and like having this in bed. They simply adore it when the woman they are in love with consents to every sex move the male performs. Every man wants a lady who is willing to experiment in bed, not one who is hesitant. And if you give him the freedom to do as he pleases, he will undoubtedly repay the favor.

7. Men do enjoy foreplay.

Ignore everything you've ever read or heard about men not enjoying foreplay online. Not all men desire to immediately jump upon penetration. Many men enjoy foreplay, and they desire it just as much as women do. If you have believed that men dislike the slow and sexy build-up, it is time to change your mind. The next time, give him enough foreplay.

8. Men also enjoy observing you while having sex.

In reality, a man needs to be in a position where he can see you becoming aroused. Men are really satisfied whenever they receive visual stimulation since they love it so much. Men find it enticing when you are in a position like a cowgirl or even a missionary where they can see you and observe your seductive reactions. Your sex sessions will be much steamier than usual since it will enrage him.

Finally, and maybe most importantly, a man wants to hear his name repeatedly in bed. For a man, there is nothing more seductive than hearing his love mutter his name!

Chapter 4

Things He Desperately Wants To Do To You In Bed

Even though many people want to experiment in the bedroom, they frequently struggle with shyness. Here is what men might be secretly pursuing.

There are many myths about what men want in the bedroom. Yes, they most likely want an oral (not a verbal) tongue-lashing. Who then doesn't?

And after seeing so much anal sex in porn, they might want to induce you.

The porn star exclaims, "Ooh that feels so good," in a fake sexy voice. "Ouch!" pops into your head.

But they also secretly desire a lot of rather "common" things. Many people simply won't ask for these since they assume it will seem ridiculous.

The following six things are what he probably wants you to do.

No. 1 Secret Sex Desire

They need you to take the initiative. So many men detest starting sex frequently. They eventually get the impression that they are putting pressure on their companion.

They genuinely want you to drop hints about how you're feeling. Or not so quietly, by grabbing them and declaring, "I want you right this second.

No. 2 Secret Sex Desire

When you "big them up" in the bedroom, men adore it.
Yes, they do desire numerous compliments throughout the act! When we consistently assume that compliment-loving women.

So tell him how much you enjoy being turned over into the doggy position. Or perhaps when he gives you a passionate kiss. Or when he amusingly performs the Full Monty strip for you in the bedroom.

No.3 Secret Sex Desire

If they remain silent during sex, respect that.
Some men become silent as they focus on reaching the climax. They probably want you to stop speaking at this point as well.

You see, some need great focus immediately before the climax.

It's a fallacy they want you yelling, "More, more, more baby!" in their ear at all points during sex.

No. 4 Secret Sex Desire

Have fun giving them or their manhood funny names.

The majority secretly adore it when you call men stuff like "Captain Stud" or give them hot nicknames for their manhood like "the jackhammer."

It's a little sex bomb that plays into how people view their sexuality. And you acknowledge seeing it.

No. 5 Secret Sex Desire

If they are not upright, avoid being direct.

Many people openly admit that they detest it when you want to have a serious conversation with them about their inability to maintain an erection, even when you're trying to be loving. or fail to raise it in the first place.
At that time, they'd much rather keep it cold. And discuss it later, not right away, while what they perceive as "failure" is still fresh in their minds.

No.6 Secret Sex Desire

Do keep their anal pleasure in mind. Numerous people openly admit that they would enjoy having some "fingertip prostate stimulation" either during foreplay or actual sex.
Suggest that by putting a condom on your finger or a latex glove on your hand, you can

tease his "forbidden" spot (or even use sturdy cling film as a barrier).

He doesn't have gay tendencies if he likes prostate stimulation, which is a ridiculous lie. Straight guys are becoming aware of the fact that it offers men incredibly strong orgasms.